KU-765-185

I Wonder Why

Camels Have Humps

and Other Questions About Animals

Anita Ganeri

Kingfisher Books

Rashida A.
T-C

Kingfisher Books, Grisewood & Dempsey Ltd,
Elsley House, 24-30 Great Titchfield Street,
London W1P 7AD

First published in 1993 by Kingfisher Books
10 9 8 7 6 5 4 3 2 1
Copyright © Grisewood & Dempsey Ltd 1993

All rights reserved. No part of this publication may
be reproduced, stored in a retrieval system or
transmitted by any means, electronic, mechanical,
photocopying or otherwise, without the prior
permission of the publisher.

BRITISH LIBRARY CATALOGUING IN PUBLICATION DATA
A catalogue record for this book is available from
the British Library

ISBN 1 85697 101 5

Phototypeset by Tradespools Ltd, Frome, Somerset
Printed and bound in Italy

Series editor: Jackie Gaff
Series designer: David West Children's Books
Author: Anita Ganeri
Consultant: Michael Chinery
Editor: Brigid Avison
Art editor: Christina Fraser
Cover illustrations: Steven Holmes (Eunice McMullen),
    cartoons by Tony Kenyon (B.L. Kearley Ltd)
Illustrations: Steven Holmes (Eunice McMullen);
    Tony Kenyon (B.L. Kearley) all cartoons.

CONTENTS

5 Which is the biggest animal?

6 What's the difference between sharks and dolphins?

8 What's the difference between frogs and toads?

8 ...and alligators and crocodiles?

9 ...and between monkeys and apes?

9 ...and rabbits and hares?

10 Why do animals have skeletons inside their bodies?

11 Which animals have skeletons on the outside?

12 Why do camels have humps?

12 Why do elephants have trunks?

13 Why do giraffes have long necks?

14 Which bird has eyes in the back of its head?

14 How do bats see in the dark?

15 Which animals smell with their tongues?

16 Why are zebras stripy?

16 Why do leopards have spots?

17 Which animal changes colour?

17 Why are flamingoes pink?

18 Why do birds have feathers?

18 Which bird can fly backwards?

19 Why can't penguins fly?

20 Which frogs can fly?

21 Which animals can walk upside down?

21 Which fish can climb trees?

22 How high can a kangaroo hop?

22 How fast can a cheetah run?

23 Which animal has an extra hand?

24 How many ants can an anteater eat?

25 Which animal uses its finger as a fork?

25 Which is the greediest animal?

26 Which animals shoot their food?

27 Which animals drink blood?

27 Which birds use fish bait?

28 Why do opossums play dead?

28 Which is the smelliest animal?

29 Which is the prickliest animal?

30 Do animals kill people?

30 Are all snakes poisonous?

31 Are all sharks dangerous?

32 Index

• Female Queen Alexandra's birdwings are the world's biggest butterflies. Their wings are almost as big as this page!

• The blue whale is so long that eight elephants could stand along its back.

Giraffe
5.5 metres tall

Elephant
3.5 metres tall
7 tonnes

Ostrich
2.5 metres tall

• The giraffe is the tallest land animal. With its long neck, it can reach as high as a two-storey house.

• The mighty African elephant is almost three times as tall as you are. It can weigh as much as seven cars.

• The ostrich is the world's tallest and heaviest bird. It's as tall as a single-decker bus!

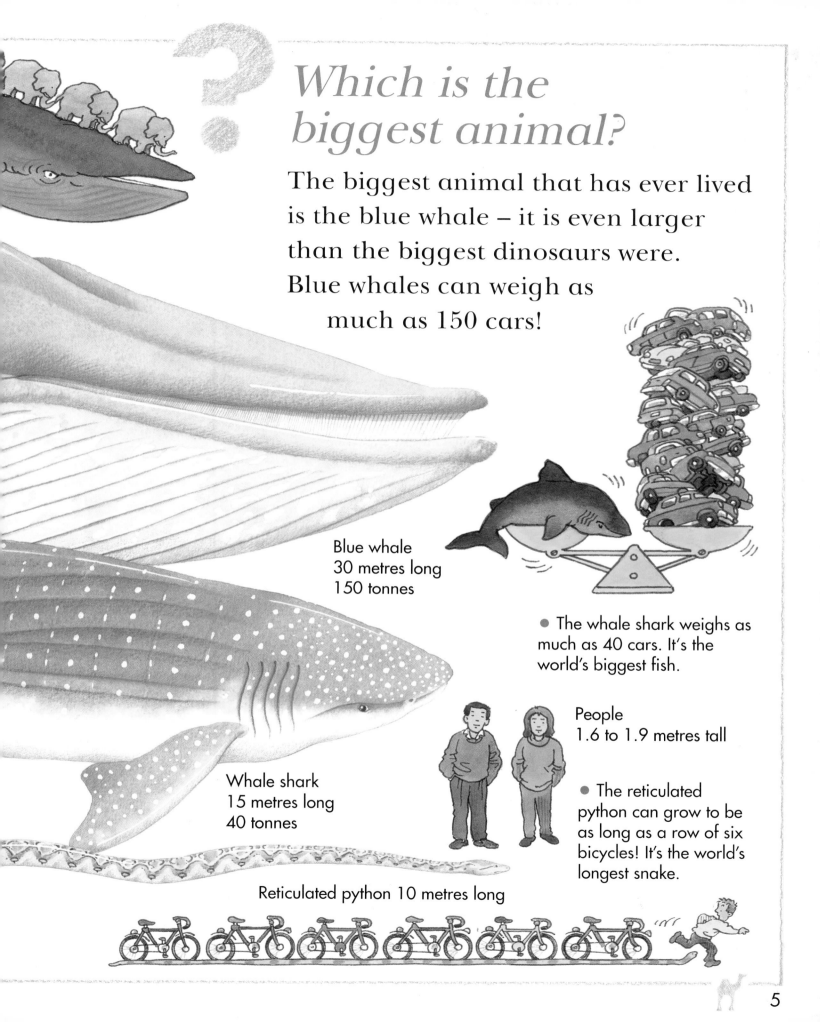

Which is the biggest animal?

The biggest animal that has ever lived is the blue whale – it is even larger than the biggest dinosaurs were. Blue whales can weigh as much as 150 cars!

Blue whale
30 metres long
150 tonnes

- The whale shark weighs as much as 40 cars. It's the world's biggest fish.

People
1.6 to 1.9 metres tall

- The reticulated python can grow to be as long as a row of six bicycles! It's the world's longest snake.

Whale shark
15 metres long
40 tonnes

Reticulated python 10 metres long

What's the difference between sharks and dolphins?

Although sharks and dolphins look alike, they belong to two very different animal groups. Sharks are a kind of fish, but dolphins are members of another group, the mammals.

● You don't look anything like a dolphin, but you are a mammal, too!

● If an animal breathes air through lungs, and its babies feed on their mother's milk, it's a mammal. Most mammals have some fur or hair on their bodies.

Lungs

● If an animal has feathers and hatches out of a hard-shelled egg, it's a bird. All birds have wings, and most of them can fly.

● If an animal has six legs and three parts to its body, it's an insect. There are more kinds of insect in the world than all the other kinds of animal put together.

Abdomen

Head

Thorax

● If an animal has damp slimy skin, and is born in water but lives much of its life on land, it's an amphibian. Baby amphibians hatch out of jelly-like eggs.

● If an animal has a dry scaly skin and is born on land, it's a reptile. Most reptiles lay eggs with leathery skins.

Scaly skin

Fin

● If an animal lives in water, breathing through gills and using fins to move, it's a fish. Most fish lay jelly-like eggs which hatch into baby fish.

Gills

What's the difference between frogs and toads?

Frogs usually have smooth skin and long legs for leaping. Most toads have lumpy skin and move their short thick bodies about by crawling.

Toad

Frog

...and alligators and crocodiles?

Crocodiles have longer, more pointed snouts than alligators. Crocodiles also have one very large tooth sticking up on each side when they close their mouths.

● Frogs and toads are both amphibians.

● Alligators and crocodiles are reptiles.

Crocodile

Alligator

...and between monkeys and apes?

The big difference between these animals is that monkeys have long tails, but apes don't have tails at all. There are lots of different kinds of monkey, but the only apes are gorillas, orang-utans, chimpanzees and gibbons.

Spider monkey

Orang-utan (ape)

● Monkeys and apes are mammals

● A woodlouse looks like it's an insect, but it isn't – it has too many legs! This creepy-crawly is related to crabs and lobsters.

● Rabbits and hares are both mammals.

...and rabbits and hares?

Hares have longer legs and ears than rabbits. Their whiskers are longer, too.

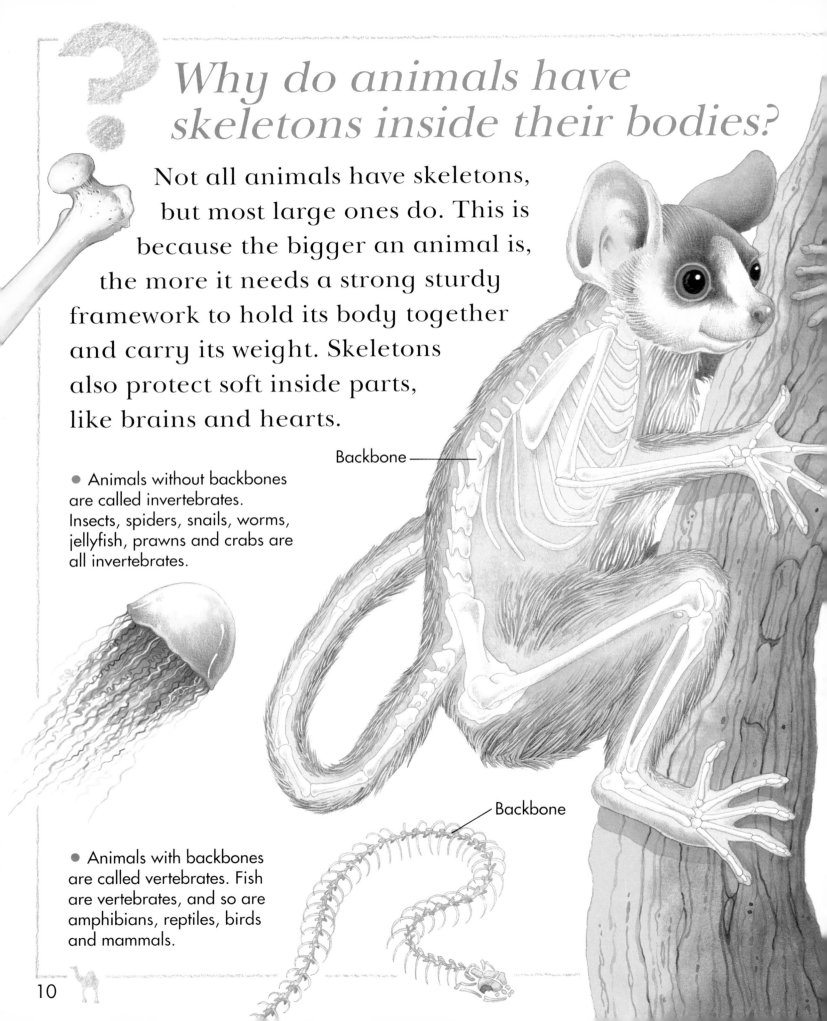

Why do animals have skeletons inside their bodies?

Not all animals have skeletons, but most large ones do. This is because the bigger an animal is, the more it needs a strong sturdy framework to hold its body together and carry its weight. Skeletons also protect soft inside parts, like brains and hearts.

Backbone —————

● Animals without backbones are called invertebrates. Insects, spiders, snails, worms, jellyfish, prawns and crabs are all invertebrates.

● Animals with backbones are called vertebrates. Fish are vertebrates, and so are amphibians, reptiles, birds and mammals.

Backbone

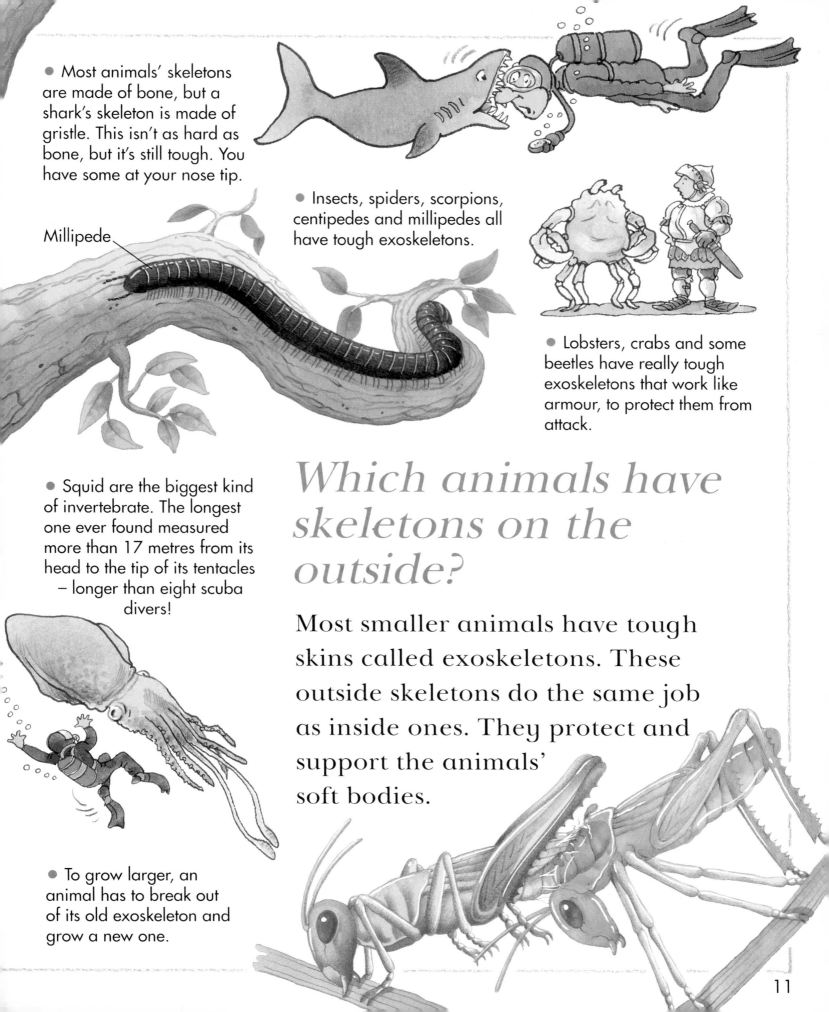

• Most animals' skeletons are made of bone, but a shark's skeleton is made of gristle. This isn't as hard as bone, but it's still tough. You have some at your nose tip.

Millipede

• Insects, spiders, scorpions, centipedes and millipedes all have tough exoskeletons.

• Lobsters, crabs and some beetles have really tough exoskeletons that work like armour, to protect them from attack.

• Squid are the biggest kind of invertebrate. The longest one ever found measured more than 17 metres from its head to the tip of its tentacles – longer than eight scuba divers!

• To grow larger, an animal has to break out of its old exoskeleton and grow a new one.

Which animals have skeletons on the outside?

Most smaller animals have tough skins called exoskeletons. These outside skeletons do the same job as inside ones. They protect and support the animals' soft bodies.

Why do camels have humps?

A camel's hump is its own built-in food cupboard. By living off the fat stored in its hump, a camel can go for as long as two weeks without eating. Camels need their humps because they live in deserts, where food and water are hard to find.

Why do elephants have trunks?

An elephant's trunk is a helpful tool. It can be used to pull down leaves and branches to eat. It also makes a good hose – elephants can squirt dust or water over themselves to keep cool.

● Elephants say 'hello' to friends by shaking trunks with them.

● An elephant's trunk is a bit like a hand. Using its tip, an elephant can pick up something as small as a button.

- Arabian camels have one hump.

- A thirsty camel can drink ten buckets of water in just 10 minutes!

- Bactrian camels have two humps.

Why do giraffes have long necks?

A giraffe's long neck makes it tall enough to eat the leaves at the top of trees. Other animals cannot reach as high, so the giraffe has lots to eat.

- A giraffe's tongue is half a metre long!

Which bird has eyes in the back of its head?

An owl's eyes aren't really in the back of its head, but at times they might as well be! Owls have such bendy necks that when they want to look backwards they swivel their heads right around!

● An owl's huge eyes help it to see at night. This is when most owls fly about hunting for food.

How do bats see in the dark?

Bats not only speed about at night without bumping into things, they also manage to hunt down juicy insects to eat. Bats can do this even when it's pitch dark, because they use sound not light to find their way.

● Bats make lots of very high squeaking sounds as they fly about. When these sounds hit objects – like insects or trees – they bounce off them, back towards the bats. The repeated sounds are called echoes. And bats can tell where things are by listening to them.